U.S. Department of Justice
Office of Justice Programs
810 Seventh Street NW.
Washington, DC 20531

John Ashcroft
Attorney General

Deborah J. Daniels
Assistant Attorney General

Richard R. Nedelkoff
Director, Bureau of Justice Assistance

Office of Justice Programs
World Wide Web Home Page
www.ojp.usdoj.gov

Bureau of Justice Assistance
World Wide Web Home Page
www.ojp.usdoj.gov/BJA

For grant and funding information contact
U.S. Department of Justice Response Center
1-800-421-6770

This project was supported by Cooperative Agreement No. 95-DD-BX-K001, awarded by the Bureau of Justice Assistance, Office of Justice Programs, U.S. Department of Justice, to Community Research Associates, Inc. This document was prepared by the Center for the Prevention of Hate Violence, University of Southern Maine, under contract with Community Research Associates, Inc. The opinions, findings, and conclusions or recommendations expressed in this document are those of the authors and do not necessarily represent the official position or policies of the U.S. Department of Justice.

The Bureau of Justice Assistance is a component of the Office of Justice Programs, which also includes the Bureau of Justice Statistics, the National Institute of Justice, the Office of Juvenile Justice and Delinquency Prevention, and the Office for Victims of Crime.

HATE CRIMES ON CAMPUS
THE PROBLEM AND EFFORTS TO CONFRONT IT

October 2001

NCJ 187249

Prepared by Stephen Wessler, Director
and Margaret Moss, Assistant Director
Center for the Prevention of Hate Violence
University of Southern Maine

Contents

I. Introduction..1

II. Hate Crimes and Bias Incidents on Campus.........................3
    Hate Crimes on Campus..3
    Bias Incidents on Campus: The Prevalence and Impact of
    Prejudice and Harassment..5

III. Response to Campus Hate Crimes and Bias Incidents..............7
    Problem 1: Campus Police Officers Need Adequate Training 7
    Problem 2: Hate Crimes and Serious Bias Incidents
    Are Not Reported..8
    Problem 3: Police Do Not Report Hate Crimes to Campus
    Administrators...9
    Problem 4: Students, Staff, and Faculty Do Not Report
    Incidents Up the Administrative Ladder..........................9
    Problem 5: Administrators Do Not Disseminate Information
    to the Campus Community......................................10

IV. Promising Efforts: Responding to and Preventing Hate Crimes.....11
    Campuswide Response to Hate Crimes..........................11
    Hate Crimes Awareness and Prevention Project.................11
    Combating Prejudice and Hate on Campus: A National
    Student Colloquium 12
    Anti-Defamation League 12
    Peer Diversity Education 12
    Campus Civility Project 13

V. Conclusion 15

VI. Appendix: Commonly Asked Questions About Hate Crimes
and Bias Incidents...17

VII. For More Information..21

I. Introduction

When a hate crime occurs on a college campus, the ideal of a university as a place for learning and growth is ruptured. Bias-motivated violence or threats targeting students, staff, or faculty not only impair the educational mission of an institution of higher learning but also deprive young men and women of the chance to live and learn in an atmosphere free of fear and intimidation. No college campus is immune to the risk of hate violence. In the past 5 years alone, the U.S. Department of Justice has brought criminal civil rights actions against students attending institutions ranging from small liberal arts colleges in Massachusetts and Georgia to large state universities in Florida and California.

This monograph examines four aspects of the problem of bias, prejudice, and hate crimes on our college and university campuses. First, the monograph examines the prevalence of hate crimes on campuses, who is targeted, what kinds of crime are committed, and the frequency and impact of bias incidents. Second, the monograph identifies common problems college communities have experienced in responding to hate crimes and provides recommendations for prompt, effective, and appropriate responses. Third, the monograph describes several promising efforts to respond to campus hate crimes and implement prevention programs. Finally, the monograph explains the difference between hate crimes and bias incidents and discusses the factors police consider to determine whether a hate crime has been committed.

II. Hate Crimes and Bias Incidents on Campus

Hate Crimes on Campus

Federal and State Enforcement Activity

Hate crimes on campuses involve a range of criminal conduct from threats to bombings to violent physical assaults. They occur at virtually every type of college and university and in every part of the nation. Perpetrators of these incidents include current and former students and nonstudents. Listed below is a sampling of recent federal and state enforcement actions involving bias-motivated violence and threats on campuses.

United States v. Samar. James Samar, a college student, was indicted on three counts of using threats of force to interfere with the federally protected rights of three students attending a small Massachusetts college. Samar used anti-Semitic slurs, threatened two fellow students, and threatened to kill one fellow student. In addition, he delivered photographs of holocaust victims to one student and stated, among other things, that the photographs were "a reminder of what happened to your relatives because they too made a mockery of Christianity." Samar entered a plea agreement.

United States v. Machado. A former student was convicted of disseminating an e-mail containing racially derogatory comments and threats to 59 college students, nearly all of whom were of Asian descent.

State v. Tozier. A student at a small college in Maine yelled anti-gay slurs and threats at a fellow student who was working in a student lounge and, in three consecutive attacks, violently choked the student. The defendant signed a consent decree in a civil rights case brought by Maine's attorney general.

United States v. Lombardi. A nonstudent was charged with detonating two pipe bombs on the campus of a primarily African-American public university in Florida. After each of the bombings, violent racist telephone calls were made to the local television station.

State v. Masotta. Three white students at a university in Maine left an anonymous racist and threatening message on an African-American student's answering machine. The message ended with the following:

> I wonder what you're gonna look like dead? Dead. I wonder if when you die you'll lose your color. Like the blood starts to

leave your body and you're gonna . . . start deteriorating and blood starts to leave your skin. . . . You get the picture? You're *** dead.

The defendants signed consent orders in a civil rights case brought by Maine's attorney general.

United States* v. *Little. The defendant, Robert Allen Little, was charged with igniting a homemade pipe bomb in the dorm room of two African-American students on a small campus in Utah. The letters "KKK" were painted in red fingernail polish on the bomb's firing device. The bomb caused extensive damage to the building and destroyed the belongings of both students. After the bombing, Little returned to the dorm and left a threatening and racist note on the door of another African-American student. Little was sentenced to 12 years in prison, fined $12,000, and ordered to pay restitution.

Campus Hate Crime Statistics

The available data on the prevalence of hate crimes and bias incidents on college campuses are not comprehensive, because they are based on information from relatively few reporting campuses. Three primary sources of data are the Federal Bureau of Investigation (FBI) Uniform Crime Reports on hate crime statistics, the U.S. Department of Education Campus Security Statistics, and the International Association of College Law Enforcement Administrators (IACLEA) annual survey on campus crime statistics.

U.S. Department of Education data are collected pursuant to the Clery Act (20 U.S.C. § 1092(f)), which was enacted in 1992. This act requires colleges and universities across the nation to report campus crimes and security policies to both the campus community and the U.S. Department of Education. In addition to policy and reporting requirements, it specifies that schools must report separately those crimes that appear to have been motivated by prejudice. The U.S. Department of Education is currently working with colleges and universities to ensure that Clery Act data are complete and current.

Even statistics based on a relatively small number of reporting schools indicate that hate crimes on campus are a significant problem. Moreover, there are strong reasons to believe that the problem of hate crimes is more widespread than any statistics are likely to reveal. First, many students, faculty, and staff members are unsure of what to report, when to report an incident, and to whom they should report an incident. Second, and perhaps most important, victims of hate crimes often are reluctant to come forward because they feel isolated and fear the potential repercussions of a perpetrator. Gay and lesbian victims who attend schools in states that do not have laws protecting individuals from job or employment discrimination based on sexual orientation may fear that reporting a hate crime will place them at risk of further discrimination. For these and other reasons, reliable statistics regarding on-campus hate crimes are elusive.

As noted above, the FBI annual compilation of hate crime statistics and IACLEA annual survey of crimes on campuses are based on data from a relatively small number of reporting institutions. The limited number of reporting institutions and the varied survey instruments also account for a disparity in the results of the two surveys. Both reports indicate, however, that many schools experience hate violence.

The Federal Bureau of Investigation Uniform Crime Report on hate crime statistics. The FBI report on 1998 hate crime statistics is based on reports from 450 colleges and universities from 40 states. Of these universities, 222 reported 241 incidents of hate crime during the year. The FBI data indicate that 57 percent of hate crimes were motivated by race, 18 percent were motivated by anti-Semitism, and 16 percent were motivated by bias based on sexual orientation.

The International Association of College Law Enforcement Administrators survey. The IACLEA report for 1998 surveyed 411 campuses. Of these campuses, 88 reported experiencing at least one hate crime; in fact, these colleges experienced an average of 3.8 hate crimes each in 1998, for a total of 334 incidents. The reporting institutions designated the motivation for the alleged hate crimes under five categories: race, religion, disability, sexual orientation, and ethnicity/national origin. The IACLEA report did not include a separate category for hate crimes motivated by bias based on gender. IACLEA statistics indicate that more than 80 percent of reported hate crimes were motivated by bias based on either race or sexual orientation.

Bias Incidents on Campus: The Prevalence and Impact of Prejudice and Harassment

Fortunately, hate crimes occur with relative infrequency on most campuses. Bias incidents (acts of prejudice that are not accompanied by violence, the threat of violence, property damage, or other illegal conduct) are far more common. Bias incidents may violate some campus disciplinary or harassment policies (making them reportable under the Clery Act), but they do not violate civil or criminal hate crime statutes.

Based on discussions, workshops, and informal surveys with hundreds of students from institutions ranging from large state universities to small liberal arts colleges, students consistently report the widespread use of degrading language and slurs by other students directed toward people of color, women, homosexuals, Jews, and others who belong to groups that have traditionally been the target of bias, prejudice, and violence. Students report hearing degrading language about women, gays, and lesbians on a daily basis and racist, anti-Semitic, and other slurs on a regular but less frequent basis.

The widespread use of degrading language and slurs directed at traditionally targeted groups has two serious consequences. First, the use of such language creates an atmosphere that permits conduct to escalate from mere words to stronger words to threats and, ultimately, to violence. In a significant portion of campus hate crime cases, the illegal conduct appears to have escalated from lower levels of harassment, beginning with degrading language. If not challenged or interrupted, the widespread use of this language sends the message—often unintended—that bias and prejudice are accepted within a campus community. Some students interpret this message to mean that more aggressive conduct may also be acceptable.

Second, even in the absence of escalation, bias incidents can have a traumatic impact on students, staff, and faculty. Members of a campus community often experience fear when they are on the receiving end of degrading language or slurs or see graffiti that targets groups in which they are members. This fear can interfere with the ability of students to fully focus on their academic work. Some students who are the target of bias-motivated harassment do not react with fear but with anger. Campus or municipal police may be called to address physical confrontations between students who are experiencing bias-motivated harassment and their harassers.

III. Response to Campus Hate Crimes and Bias Incidents

The responses of campus administrators and campus and municipal police departments to hate crimes and bias incidents that occur on college campuses have varied greatly. Although there is no one correct way to handle every hate crime, the direct experiences of police officers and administrators make it possible to identify common problems they encounter in responding to campus hate crimes and those responses that permit effective investigation and appropriate community response.

Some of the most common problems in responding to hate crimes are that police are inadequately trained; students, staff, faculty, and administrators do not report the crimes; and administrators do not adequately disseminate information to the campus community. Listed below are descriptions of common problems, followed by recommended steps for effectively dealing with these frequently encountered challenges.

Problem 1: Campus Police Officers Need Adequate Training

Campus police officers who have not been trained to identify and respond to hate crimes may not be prepared to properly investigate incidents and recognize potential ramifications for the safety of students on campus. In addition, if police officers do not identify an act of campus violence as a possible hate crime and do not report it to the administration, the college or university may be hampered in its efforts to identify trends and begin appropriate prevention and intervention work.

Recommendations

Implement a training program for campus police. It is essential that all members of campus police departments (and municipal police departments that have colleges or universities within their jurisdictions) receive training in responding to and investigating hate crimes. All officers within a department, including command officers, patrol officers, and detectives, should attend training sessions. Police departments have an array of training programs available to them. In 1998, the U.S. Department of Justice launched its National Hate Crime Training Initiative. This initiative developed curricula for training police officers in how to respond to and investigate hate crimes and convened national train-the-trainer conferences around the nation. The initiative has taught trainers in every state to conduct half- or full-day courses. Additionally, the Bureau of

Justice Assistance has developed a 20-minute training film for officers, titled *Responding to Hate Crimes,* and the International Association of Chiefs of Police has developed a 12-page guide for officers that covers the major components of investigating and responding to hate crimes.

Designate a civil rights officer for each department. Every campus and municipal police department with colleges located within its jurisdiction should consider appointing at least one officer (preferably two) to serve as the designated civil rights officer. A designated civil rights officer is the primary liaison between campus administration, advocacy groups, and other law enforcement agencies (including prosecutorial offices). Appointing a designated civil rights officer lets the entire campus community know that responding to and investigating hate crimes is a priority, and hate crimes will be handled in a coordinated and consistent way. For more information about designating a civil rights officer, see *Addressing Hate Crimes: Six Initiatives That Are Enhancing the Efforts of Criminal Justice Practitioners* (February 2000, Bureau of Justice Assistance Hate Crimes Series).

Problem 2: Hate Crimes and Serious Bias Incidents Are Not Reported

Police believe that students, staff, faculty, and administrators often do not report possible hate crimes and serious bias incidents to the police. If police are not informed promptly of a possible hate crime, they cannot conduct an immediate investigation. As a result, physical evidence (such as graffiti or recorded telephone messages) may be lost, and witnesses may not be identified and interviewed. The nonreporting of such incidents is particularly serious because many perpetrators of hate crimes repeat and escalate their behavior until they are confronted by authorities. Consequently, police are deprived of information that may enable them to halt this pattern of escalation before a more serious crime is committed.

Recommendation

Campus officials should develop a brochure that defines what should be reported, to whom an incident should be reported, and when an incident should be reported. The brochure should provide clear directives and be distributed broadly to faculty, staff, and students. It is particularly important that these brochures be distributed to those persons on campus who are most likely to learn about possible hate crimes. For example, individuals working for the campus housing and athletics departments, including student life staff, resident advisors, coaches, and team captains, should all receive and review the reporting guidelines. Student leaders throughout the university community, whether or not they are directly involved with the housing or athletics departments, should also receive and review reporting guidelines.

The Recommendation section under Problem 4 sets forth guidelines.

Problem 3: Police Do Not Report Hate Crimes to Campus Administrators

Some law enforcement agencies may not have a procedure for regularly informing college administrators of hate crimes or serious bias incidents that occur in or around a college campus, particularly when incidents occur on campus but not in campus housing. Inadequate reporting of such incidents by police deprives administrators of the opportunity to support students from the affected or targeted groups, provide reasonable warnings to members of the campus community, and put prevention efforts in place.

Recommendation

Campuses should provide both campus and municipal police departments with clear and specific guidelines denoting who at the university or college should be contacted and under what circumstances. The reporting guidelines must be concise, identifying who should receive an initial report and who should receive followup information. The guidelines should include information on how to contact these individuals in the evening and on weekends, during campus holidays, and during vacations to avoid lapses in reporting.

Problem 4: Students, Staff, and Faculty Do Not Report Incidents Up the Administrative Ladder

When students, staff, and faculty do not report (or do not report in a timely manner) possible hate crimes or serious bias incidents up the administrative ladder, senior college officials are denied critical information. If senior administrators are unaware of possible hate crimes, they will not be prepared to take action against perpetrators, initiate preventive measures, or respond knowledgeably to community and press inquiries.

Recommendation

Campus administrators should work with campus and municipal police to develop and disseminate clear guidelines for reporting hate crimes. The guidelines should address the following:

- When and under what circumstances students, staff, and faculty should report hate crimes and bias incidents to campus or municipal police.

- When and under what circumstances students, staff, and faculty should report hate crimes and bias incidents to college administrators.

- When campus and municipal police should report hate crimes and bias incidents to college administrators.

The guidelines should include the names of individuals to contact during the week, as well as in the evenings, on weekends, and during campus holidays and vacations.

Problem 5: Administrators Do Not Disseminate Information to the Campus Community

When a hate crime occurs on campus, information about the incident spreads quickly throughout the campus community via informal avenues of communication. If college or university administrators do not inform the campus about the incident, several adverse consequences can occur. First, students, staff, and faculty may receive inaccurate information about what occurred. Second, the institution will lose the opportunity to send a strong message that bias and hate will not be tolerated on campus. Finally, and often most destructive, when college administrators do not publicly comment on hate crimes, they may inadvertently create the impression that the institution is insensitive to the problem of hate crimes.

Recommendations

Disseminate information about hate crimes. Senior college and university administrators should consider promptly disseminating information through a campuswide letter or e-mail to provide details on alleged hate crimes and to strongly condemn bias-motivated violence, threats, and property damage. Often, it will be appropriate to follow this communication with an open campus meeting at which members of the campus community can ask questions and express their views. Campus disciplinary proceedings generally are confidential; therefore, any dissemination of information should take confidentiality restrictions into account.

Establish a hate crime response team. Administrators may want to establish a hate crime response team that recommends when and how the college or university should respond to an alleged hate crime. Hate crime response teams should include representatives from the president's office, the dean of students office, the multicultural office, the equal opportunity employer office, and campus and municipal police departments.

IV. Promising Efforts: Responding to and Preventing Hate Crimes

Colleges, universities, and nonprofit organizations are developing innovative ways to respond to and prevent hate crimes. The efforts described below are only a few examples of the creative programs being implemented around the nation to make our institutions of higher learning safe for all students. These programs are replicable and generally can be implemented without significant expense.

Campuswide Response to Hate Crimes

Many colleges and universities have responded to hate crimes on their campuses with a broad-based public condemnation of bias, prejudice, and violence. These responses have included the following:

- An open letter from the college or university president or dean to the campus community that explains the hate crime or bias incident that occurred on campus, the status of the police investigation of the alleged hate crime, and a strong condemnation of bias and violence.

- Meetings open to the entire campus community in which the president and other senior administrators explain what has occurred and restate the university's position against hate crimes. Students, staff, and faculty often are invited to ask questions and voice their opinions.

As a result of these and other actions, college administrators have calmed tensions and fears; addressed the need of students, staff, and faculty to receive reliable information; and gained the trust and confidence of the campus community.

Hate Crimes Awareness and Prevention Project

Students at the University of California at Berkeley have developed a project to examine hate crimes and the underlying issues of bias and prejudice. Through education and training the project has increased awareness of the threat of hate crimes and fostered a campus climate that discourages hate crimes. The project includes a Web site that provides options for reporting hate crimes and lists additional campus and community resources. The project sponsored a Hate Crimes Awareness Week in spring 2000.

Combating Prejudice and Hate on Campus: A National Student Colloquium

In March 2000, the Brudnick Center on Violence and Conflict at Northeastern University and the Center for the Prevention of Hate Violence at the University of Southern Maine cosponsored a national student colloquium to recognize those students, and their respective campus organizations, who are working to confront bias, hate, and violence. The event provided the students with the opportunity to build skills and learn from each other. More than 300 students and staff from more than 70 campuses throughout the country attended the colloquium. The colloquium was funded and supported by the U.S. Department of Education's Safe and Drug-Free Schools Program and the Bureau of Justice Assistance, U.S. Department of Justice.

Anti-Defamation League

The Anti-Defamation League (ADL) formed its World of Difference Institute in 1992 to "define and advance a discipline of diversity education." The institute's Campus of Difference Program provides training for students in groups of 25–40. Facilitated by two ADL staff members, the program's goal is to increase awareness of bias incidents and hate crimes and encourage university students to make proactive changes on campus. The Campus of Difference Program also offers train-the-trainer sessions of varying duration that enable a campus to develop 16–20 diversity trainers.

Peer Diversity Education

Several schools have implemented peer diversity education groups that promote understanding of diversity on campus. At Texas A&M University, University Awareness for Cultural Togetherness (U–ACT) is a peer diversity education group that requires participating students to take a semester-long course in social justice issues in higher education. Members of the group then conduct workshops and hold overnight retreats in an effort to bring students together and create an environment that is "safe, supportive, and educational."

New Jersey City University's Peers Educating Peers, or "PEP," program is based in the school's psychology department. About 25 students actively participate in PEP; they provide outreach on campus and to the community on a variety of issues. Other schools, including Bowdoin College in Maine and the University of Denver in Colorado, have successfully integrated peer diversity efforts into freshman orientation, using films, small group discussions, and campus speakers to increase awareness and promote safety.

Campus Civility Project

The Center for the Prevention of Hate Violence at the University of Southern Maine has initiated the Campus Civility Project to address the climate of bias, prejudice, and harassment that exists on our nation's campuses. Administrators, faculty, staff, and student leaders (such as resident advisors and captains of sports teams) participate in 3-hour workshops that help them develop a fuller understanding of the harmful effects of degrading language and slurs. Most important, the workshops also provide participants with practical skills for intervening in low-key ways when students engage in conduct that demeans, degrades, or frightens others. The center conducts a 3-day training-of-trainers conference for representatives from each participating campus that will enable the campuses to conduct their own workshops for student leaders, staff, and faculty year after year.

V. Conclusion

The hate crimes and bias incidents that occur on this nation's college and university campuses not only leave scars on the targeted individuals but also on entire campuses. College administrators, police officers, students, and faculty members around the nation are devoting energy and creativity to responding to and preventing bias, prejudice, and hate violence. The cumulative impact of this work on campus will help ensure that all students—regardless of gender, race/ethnicity, sexual orientation, disability, religion, or age—are physically and emotionally safe.

VI. Appendix: Commonly Asked Questions About Hate Crimes and Bias Incidents

What Is a Hate Crime?

The Federal Government, more than 40 states, and the District of Columbia have hate crime statutes. These statutes vary in a number of ways. Generally, a hate crime is a crime of violence, property damage, or threat that is motivated in whole or in part by an offender's bias based on race, religion, ethnicity, national origin, gender, physical or mental disability, or sexual orientation. Most jurisdictions that have hate crime laws cover bias based on race, religion, ethnicity, and national origin, and a smaller number of states cover bias based on gender, disability, and sexual orientation.

In addition to criminal statutes, many states have civil statutes that authorize the state attorney general to seek restraining orders against persons who engage in bias-motivated violence, threats, or property damage. It is important to check the exact wording of the hate crime statutes applicable in your state.

What Are Hate or Bias Incidents?

Hate or bias incidents involve behavior that is motivated by bias based on race, religion, ethnicity, national origin, gender, disability, or sexual orientation. These incidents do not involve criminal conduct such as assault, threats, or property damage. Bias-motivated degrading comments often are considered to be bias incidents. They are not considered to be hate crimes, however, because the speaker of those comments has not engaged in criminal activity.

Why Do We Need To Focus on This Issue?

Police officers and prosecutors have learned that hate crimes can occur on any campus—urban or rural, large or small, public or private. Police and prosecutors have found that the lack of reported hate crimes only indicates that students, staff, or faculty are not reporting incidents, not that hate crimes are absent. Moreover, even if a campus has not experienced a reported hate crime, it is likely that students and other members of the campus community are hearing and using degrading language and slurs directed at those on campus who are of a different race, religion, gender, or sexual orientation. A campus culture in which the use of slurs becomes commonplace and accepted soon becomes an environment in which slurs can escalate to harassment, harassment can escalate to threats, and threats can escalate to physical violence. As noted previously in this monograph, an act of violence is the end result of this pattern. Even if violence does not occur, the degrading language alone has a negative impact on certain students, causing some to feel uncomfortable or unaccepted and others to feel scared.

How Do Police Officers Determine Whether a Hate Crime Has Occurred?

Police officers are trained to examine whether bias indicators exist. A bias crime indicator is an objective fact, circumstance, or pattern—standing alone or in conjunction with other facts or circumstances—that suggests that the offender's actions were motivated, in whole or in part, by bias. The presence of bias indicators does not establish that a hate crime has occurred. Rather, the presence of bias indicators prompts police to investigate the matter further to determine its motivation. The following factors may indicate bias motivation. Each factor is followed by one or more examples of bias indicators.

Racial, ethnic, gender, and cultural differences exist between the perpetrator and victim.

- The racial identity, religion, ethnic/national origin, disability, or sexual orientation of the victim differs from that of the offender.

- The victim is a member of a group that is overwhelmingly outnumbered by members of another group in the area where the incident occurred.

- The victim was engaged in activities promoting his or her group.

- The incident coincided with a holiday or date of particular significance to the victim's group.

Comments, written statements, and gestures were made. Bias-related comments, written statements, or gestures were made by the offender either during, before, or after the alleged hate crime.

Drawings, markings, symbols, and graffiti were left. Bias-related drawings, markings, symbols, or graffiti were left at the scene of the incident.

Organized hate groups or their members were involved. A hate group has claimed responsibility for the crime, or symbols of organized

Appendix: Commonly Asked Questions About Hate Crimes and Bias Incidents

hate groups were left at the crime scene.

The victim previously had received bias-motivated harassing mail or phone calls. Several bias-motivated incidents have occurred in the same area.

The victim's or witness's perception of the incident may affect the outcome. Victims or witnesses believe that the incident was motivated by bias.

The location of the incident indicates bias motivation.

- The victim was in or near a place commonly associated with or frequented by individuals of a particular racial identity, religion, ethnic/national origin, disability, sexual orientation, or gender.

- The incident occurred at or near a place of worship, a religious cemetery, the home of a family that is a minority within a particular neighborhood, or a gay bar.

Can a Hate Crime Be Committed With Nothing More Than Words?

The use of bigoted and prejudiced language does not in itself violate hate crime laws. This type of behavior is frequently classified as a bias incident. However, hate crime laws apply when words threaten violence. Similarly, hate crime laws apply when bias-motivated graffiti damages or destroys property.

Does Bias Have To Be the Only Motivation To Charge Someone With a Hate Crime?

In general, no, although the answer may depend on how courts in a particular jurisdiction or state have interpreted hate crime laws. It is not uncommon for people to commit crimes for more than one reason. Many hate crimes are successfully prosecuted even when motivations in addition to bias are present.

Is Domestic Violence or Sexual Assault Against a Woman Considered a Hate Crime?

Domestic violence or sexual assault can be prosecuted as a hate crime if gender is included in applicable hate crime laws and if evidence can be obtained demonstrating that the assault was motivated, in whole or in part, by bias against the victim because of her gender.

Do Hate Crime Laws Protect White People?

Yes. Hate crime laws are color-blind. Racially motivated crimes targeting white people, although far less common than hate crimes targeting people of color, occur and the perpetrators are prosecuted. Many of the hate crimes motivated by bias against a victim's religion, nationality, gender, or sexual orientation are directed at white people.

Do Victims Frequently Fabricate Hate Crimes?

As with any crime, fabricated complaints about hate crimes do occur, but very rarely. In fact, police have found that victims often are reluctant to report hate crimes or even acknowledge that what appears to others to be a hate crime is motivated by bias. The fear and isolation that hate crime victims feel lead to underreporting more often than to fabrication.

Why Should These Laws Protect Homosexuals?

Hate crime laws prohibit violence, threats, or property damage motivated by bias. Hate crime laws have always applied to people who choose to be in a targeted group, such as those who choose to convert to a different religion. The resolution of the debate over whether gays and lesbians are genetically predisposed or choose their sexual orientation is not relevant under the law. No person should be subject to violence, threats, or property damage because of his or her status, whether it be race, ethnicity, nationality, religion, gender, physical or mental disability, or sexual orientation.

Do Hate Crime Laws Confer Special Rights on Certain Groups?

Hate crime laws protect every person in this country. Anyone could be a victim of a hate crime because of his or her race, nationality, ethnicity, physical or mental disability, sexual orientation, gender, or religion. Some people have been victimized by hate crimes due to a perpetrator's mistaken belief that the victim is of a particular race, nationality, ethnicity, or sexual orientation. Hate crimes do not confer special rights on anyone. Rather, they protect the rights of individuals to conduct their everyday activities—to live in their homes, do their jobs, receive an education—without being subjected to violence because of who they are or what they believe.

VII. For More Information

To learn more about the programs discussed in this monograph, please contact the following organization:

Center for the Prevention of Hate Violence
University of Southern Maine
96 Falmouth Street
P.O. Box 9300
Portland, ME 04104
207-780-4756
Fax: 207-780-5698
Web site: www.cphv.usm.maine.edu
E-mail: cphv@usm.maine.edu

For additional copies of this monograph and others in BJA's Hate Crimes Series, contact:

Bureau of Justice Assistance Clearinghouse
P.O. Box 6000
Rockville, MD 20849-6000
1-800-688-4252
Fax: 301-519-5212
Web site: www.ncjrs.org

Clearinghouse staff are available Monday through Friday, 8:30 a.m. to 7 p.m. eastern time. Ask to be placed on the BJA mailing list.

For information from other organizations that are addressing hate crimes, please contact any of the organizations listed below.

Anti-Defamation League
823 United Nations Plaza
New York, NY 10017
212-490-2525
Web site: www.adl.org

Arab American Institute
1600 K Street NW., Suite 601
Washington, DC 20006
202-429-9210
Fax: 202-429-9214
Web site: www.aaiusa.org

Bureau of Justice Assistance
810 Seventh Street NW.
Washington, DC 20531
202-616-6500
Fax: 202-305-1367
Web site: www.ojp.usdoj.gov/bja

Bureau of Justice Statistics
810 Seventh Street NW.
Washington, DC 20531
202-307-0765
Fax: 202-307-5846
Web site: www.ojp.usdoj.gov/bjs

Community Relations Service
U.S. Department of Justice
600 E Street NW., Suite 6000
Washington, DC 20530
202-305-2935
Fax: 202-305-3009
Web site: www.usdoj.gov/crs

Disability Law Center
11 Beacon Street, Suite 925
Boston, MA 02108
617-723-8455
Fax: 617-723-9125
Web site: www.dlc-ma.org

Facing History and Ourselves National Foundation
16 Hurd Road
Brookline, MA 02445
617–232–1595
Fax: 617–232–0281
Web site: www.facinghistory.org

Federal Bureau of Investigation
J. Edgar Hoover Building
935 Pennsylvania Avenue NW.
Washington, DC 20535
202–324–3000
Fax: 202–324–5310
Web site: www.fbi.gov

Federal Bureau of Investigation
Criminal Justice Information Services Division
Attn: Uniform Crime Reports
1000 Custer Hollow Road
Clarksburg, WV 26306
304–625–4995
Fax: 304–625–5394
Web site: www.fbi.gov/ucr/ucr.htm

Human Rights Campaign
919 18th Street NW., Suite 800
Washington, DC 20006
202–628–4160
Fax: 202–347–5323
Web site: www.hrc.org

International Association of Chiefs of Police
515 North Washington Street
Alexandria, VA 22314–2357
703–836–6767
Fax: 703–836–4543
Web site: www.theiacp.org

National Asian Pacific American Legal Consortium
1140 Connecticut Avenue NW., Suite 1200
Washington, DC 20036
202–296–2300
Fax: 202–296–2318
Web site: www.napalc.org

National Conference for Community and Justice
475 Park Avenue South, 19th Floor
New York, NY 10016
212–545–1300
Fax: 212–545–8053
Web site: www.nccj.org

National Congress of American Indians
1301 Connecticut Avenue NW., Suite 200
Washington, DC 20036
202–466–7767
Fax: 202–466–7797
Web site: www.ncai.org

National Council of La Raza
1111 19th Street NW., Suite 1000
Washington, DC 20036
202–785–1670
Fax: 202–776–1792
Web site: www.nclr.org

National Criminal Justice Association
444 North Capitol Street NW., Suite 618
Washington, DC 20001
202–624–1440
Fax: 202–508–3859
Web site: www.ncja.org

For More Information

National Gay and Lesbian Task Force
1700 Kalorama Road NW., Suite 101
Washington, DC 20009
202-332-6483
Fax: 202-332-0207
Web site: www.ngltf.org

National Partnership for Women and Families
1875 Connecticut Avenue NW., Suite 710
Washington, DC 20009
202-986-2600
Fax: 202-986-2539
Web site: www.nationalpartnership.org

National Women's Law Center
11 Dupont Circle NW., Suite 800
Washington, DC 20036
202-588-5180
Fax: 202-588-5185
Web site: www.nwlc.org

Network of Violence Prevention Practitioners
55 Chapel Street
Newton, MA 02458
617-969-7100
Fax: 617-244-3436
Web site: www2.edc.org/nvpp

Office of Juvenile Justice and Delinquency Prevention
810 Seventh Street NW.
Washington, DC 20531
202-307-5911
Fax: 202-307-2093
Web site: www.ojjdp.ncjrs.org

Office for Victims of Crime
810 Seventh Street NW.
Washington, DC 20531
202-307-5983
Fax: 202-514-6383
Web site: www.ojp.usdoj.gov/ovc

Simon Wiesenthal Center
1399 South Roxbury Drive
Los Angeles, CA 90035
310-553-9036
Fax: 310-553-8007
Web site: www.wiensenthal.com

U.S. Commission on Civil Rights
624 Ninth Street NW., Suite 700
Washington, DC 20425
202-337-7700
Fax: 202-376-7558
Web site: www.usccr.gov

U.S. Department of Education
Safe and Drug-Free Schools
400 Maryland Avenue SW.
Washington, DC 20202
202-260-3954
Fax: 202-260-7767
Web site: www.ed.gov

U.S. Department of Housing and Urban Development
451 Seventh Street SW.
Washington, DC 20410
202-708-2111
Fax: 202-619-8365
Web site: www.hud.gov

U.S. Department of Justice
Civil Rights Division, Criminal Section
601 D Street NW.
Washington, DC 20530
202-514-3204
Fax: 202-514-8336
Web site: www.usdoj.gov

Violence Against Women Office
810 Seventh Street NW.
Washington, DC 20531
202–307–6026
Fax: 202–305–2589
Web site: www.ojp.usdoj.gov/vawo

For additional information about BJA programs, visit the BJA Web site at www.ojp.usdoj.gov/bja or contact:

Bureau of Justice Assistance Clearinghouse
P.O. Box 6000
Rockville, MD 20849–6000
1–800–688–4252
Web site: www.ncjrs.org

Clearinghouse staff are available Monday through Friday, 8:30 a.m. to 7 p.m. eastern time. Ask to be placed on the BJA mailing list.

U.S. Department of Justice Response Center
1–800–421–6770 or 202–307–1480

Response Center staff are available Monday through Friday, 9 a.m. to 5 p.m. eastern time.

Bureau of Justice Assistance Information

General Information

Callers may contact the U.S. Department of Justice Response Center for general information or specific needs, such as assistance in submitting grant applications and information about training. To contact the Response Center, call 1–800–421–6770 or write to 1100 Vermont Avenue NW., Washington, DC 20005.

Indepth Information

For more indepth information about BJA, its programs, and its funding opportunities, requesters can call the BJA Clearinghouse. The BJA Clearinghouse, a component of the National Criminal Justice Reference Service (NCJRS), shares BJA program information with state and local agencies and community groups across the country. Information specialists are available to provide reference and referral services, publication distribution, participation and support for conferences, and other networking and outreach activities. The Clearinghouse can be reached by

- ❏ **Mail**
  P.O. Box 6000
  Rockville, MD 20849–6000

- ❏ **Visit**
  2277 Research Boulevard
  Rockville, MD 20850

- ❏ **Telephone**
  1–800–688–4252
  Monday through Friday
  8:30 a.m. to 7 p.m.
  eastern time

- ❏ **Fax**
  301–519–5212

- ❏ **Fax on Demand**
  1–800–688–4252

- ❏ **BJA Home Page**
  www.ojp.usdoj.gov/BJA

- ❏ **NCJRS Home Page**
  www.ncjrs.org

- ❏ **E-mail**
  askncjrs@ncjrs.org

- ❏ **JUSTINFO Newsletter**
  E-mail to listproc@ncjrs.org
  Leave the subject line blank
  In the body of the message, type:
  subscribe justinfo
  [your name]

www.ingramcontent.com/pod-product-compliance
Lightning Source LLC
Chambersburg PA
CBHW061522180526
45171CB00001B/292